SHUT UP SHED

Julie Coltherd Shaw

To order additional copies of this book, contact:
Xlibris
1-888-795-4274
www.Xlibris.com
Orders@Xlibris.com

Contents

Shut Up Shed

I hear the birds chirp,
I watch the boats slowly cross over the sound,
I see the wind, its actually talking thru the trees today. But somethings trying to interupt this tranquil day - when I look around I see wood on the grass in my yard, old bones, dead flowers here & there - close by in my perefrial I see the shed

Shovels, gloves, rakes, trash bags ect inside. My shed says stop sitting on the riverside

when the yards a mess - come get this rake & pick up the yard -
Shut up shed, (I say) as another boat slowly passes and I sip my tea -

Imagine This

Why are you always there, interupting my every single thought
Getting all my attention - Silence - - - - -
I am not hearing you today, are you in there
My moment, my silent moment, silence interupted
I knew you would return its, torment, its deviant, and discusting
I IGNORE!!!
Silence......
Are you gone, for now
Your torment has slowly whinned down to a whispering annoying ringing
in my ear -
My sweet silent moment
Once more.
To become free of its tourment
I want to be free

Axe to Grind

The pavement I drive on, the gasoline, I power my car with, the people in the very town I live in. The money I give the cashier - the fountain drink at McDonalds

The clothes on my back - I've wanted short hair now for over a year - I want to stop cleaning - I dont want to be responsible for some one else's happiness.

Cooking each evening - cleaning each day. Doing my make up- putting laundry away. Listening to my husbands delemas - I know he works so hard so he keeps going each morning. To do the same job.

Im screaming out get me out of here I'm thru with this grind. Its not what Im supposed to be doing. I should cut all my hair off good n short - stop shopping. I dont need any thing more. Wearing makup maybe Ill keep doing that.

I'm winking at 50 but I feel young enough to start a new life. I'm afraid of everthing I dont have courage to walk away from this life to start a new uncertain one.

Alaska where there's wide open spaces and no axe to grind its a dream I'm having just for a year - just drop what Im doing buy a ticket get off the plane and head to Hoonah, then what be a begger.

I'm screaming to get away, silently

???

Bestie

When your best friend puts his head on your lap and looks up at you, and you look directly into his eyes -

I say ok you can stay! But' only 5 minites. You share a patio lounger as the hot sun emerges from behind the grey clouds - Bestie gets more comfortable as you roll your eyes, the slight breeze brings a scent to the air - not sure what it might be.

Bestie follows it, points his nose straigh out and the afternoon loung is all mine again. Did I mention my best-friend is a fox red Labradore 120 lbs - the scent was a little baby bird or 4 in the nest behind the house.

Tea Cups & Saucers

I love my tea cups & saucers,

Ohh - that thin little rim the light weight of this little cup its quaint small finger hole. Ohh teacups & saucers, how you bring warmth to me, an instant sip becomes pure indulgane in this moment - and the next. An impulse, (I want tea)

Within 1 moment there you are sitting on your saucer beautifully painted sitting erect, and always ready to please me.

Your lovely round perfect saucer, holds all my favorate biscuts chocolates, sometimes just a thumb. Let this become our time, one more time besides its only 10 a.m.

Busy Body

Nosey, busybodies, step outside there own lives and uninvitedly step into someone elses.

Rumors, start, people talking, the ugly whispering, the tortures questions.

Busy bodies are clueless the damage they cause the heckeling they create. This termoil inside the very circle in wich were co existing.

I say busy body its time to say good night.

Take her hand and walk her to your door. Open it then.

Shut it with busy body on other side.

Awww, peace at last.

7500

Absolutley no filter there are no boundaries here, or any where in this life. These steps will never colaps, its secured with nails and strong wood.

I never felt guilt, or shame, apologetic never remorseful. I, am strong here, not weak.

My heart is a see of open waters, no secrets here.

Until I was corrected. Now 7500 times No.

Open Up

Its always there once you have had it, or found it.

Its dwelling deeply down in this small body of skin & bones. The inner being longs to feel it forever like a drug.

Love never fails, its enormous ocean of feeling's just runs as though a stream in an open peice of Alaskan wilderness no one knows about.

Its forgiving, and also it can be pain - more pain than a person's heart can truely overcome. Because you never get over a once perfectly molded unbroken, now broken heart.

Its compassionate it cares it worries, love is so many emotions mostley its freedom when with the one love is freedom

Cloudy Days Are Going Away

A cloudy day comes an goes in this place.

Dark, cold silent no voices but my own thoughts ohhhh, this place.

The grey clouds are an eternity of Love lost friendships ending, oneself, forgotten, inner peice gone!! Like an Alaskan short summer - to become ice cold winter wich seems endless

Where? Where will life take me, where will all my mistakes lead my pathetic life

I must intervine my own misery, (shut up) I tell myself

Do something, theres a long slope down before you come up - I want out I whisper I'm getting out.

Indiana Jones

She's just right, in all the ways a woman needs her to be.

I enjoy her personality its very positive, embracing all your juvinile topics, love, religion, family, n hobbies.

She is a woman of many talents, adventouros and couragous, my fearful nature entises her to become my Indiana Jones

I love that in her.

She is very smart, loves her family, she loves her mother, her sister, her stepfather she speaks of with respect.

She is everything good,

I see me in her an her me, I know this is good

A friendship worth going for I know your worth it

Imprint

When our Lord up above puts something on your heart it is imprinted there for all eternity.

Even the blackest of souls, untouched by goodness can not fight this.

My heart says go on and live, live free with no concience no enemy shall ever form against me! So I do live free.

God has given all who choose it freedom, reach out and grab it, its ours to choose

Forgiveness is a choice its my freedom to live in this one life on this beautiful earth free.

From emotional imprisonment, or a blackened soul for ever this is imprinted on my heart. And I choose to forgive to be free

The Dream

Those brown discusting roaches. Up the walls, in the cabinets, on my food
The food we eat. The beds we sleep in
Spray spray spray there running n running away, constantly - only to a resolve short lived
Morning runs consist of running away from bugs, big enough to carry a slipper off

I hear a mans voice its saying come with me, Ill change all this, just trust.
Who are you I say, how can you possibly take four people away and change things here. I can he replies.
And I will and he did.
Did I mention I havent seen a cockroach in 17 years.

Elbows on the Table

When in his presence your safe, he protects you with his life as you look in his eye's you see pride and you see love - when he holds you near all troubles vinish as tho a salmon berry bush in Alaska in the month of September all is aliened with him nothing can touch you, no harm no pain or hurt. As years pass he teaches you, to be a strong woman and a lady. Be proper he says, as he knocks your elbows off the table. I love you Boo - those words are tattooed in my memory for ever. Before you were snatched away from this earth, you told me you loved me. I still feel your breath in my left ear - we were slow dancing to old lang syne New Years Eve you are my light you guide the way. I love you Dad

???

1.9 Miles

My road home is 1.9 miles from the drive way.

Tree tops touch one another from opposite sides of the little narrow road. Brush is over grown and rabbits dash in and out of traffict. (Buy traffic I mean the one or two odd cars coming or going.

A little doe has lost its mother she is light brown with a little whistle white tail it sticks straight up like a door handle jammed and rusted there

She is a sweet and curious little thing. Three little mice live in my yard they dig more holes and make large mounds of dirt as if a beaver dillagently building her dam! We have a snake to he's in our bushes after escaping out of the pond.

A bald eagle found a home in our highest tree his partner has gone and left him all alone. Creatures are pretty active around here around my house. And I hope to see them around for a while so I can make some new friends

???

It Must Be 8 o'clock

Finding myself on the sound - I can hear the wind its very loud this day.

The limbs on the trees are blowing back n forth as tho a ship on a sailing expedition on its windiest of days. The water is rippling past in a steady even motion - almost fast forward -

Finding myself on the sound, all alone not a person for miles, enjoying my own company, listening to my own thoughts, writing them down on this little pad with this pen.

I hear a little airaplane approching 10000 feet up above my tranquil house, the bee's are buzzing around in the rose garden 30 feet from my ear, the sky is grey an blue, dusk is approaching - it must be 8 o'clock

This earth is so beautiful
I thank God for this beautiful place.
As my pad runs out of paper I must go, so I go.